Butterfly Haiku Coloring Book

By

Jacquelyn Jaie Fourgerel

_____

_____

_____

_____

_____

_____

_____

_____

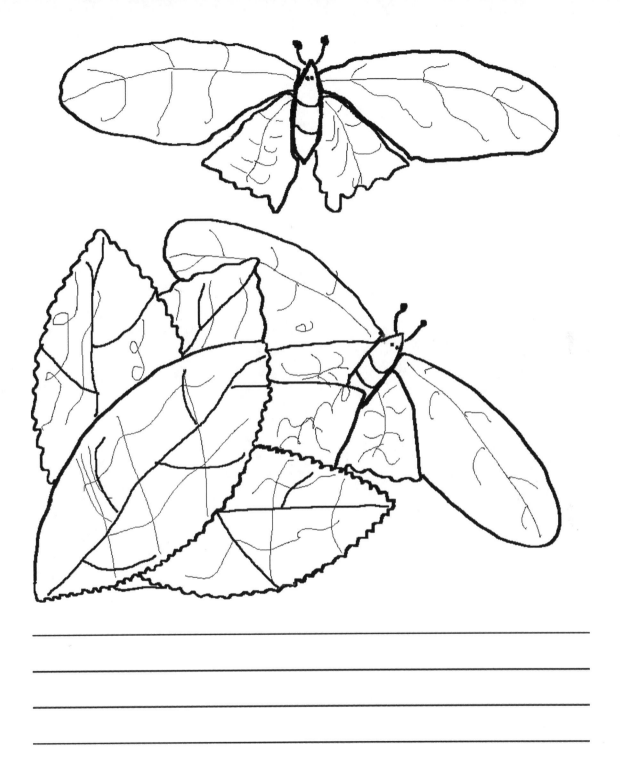

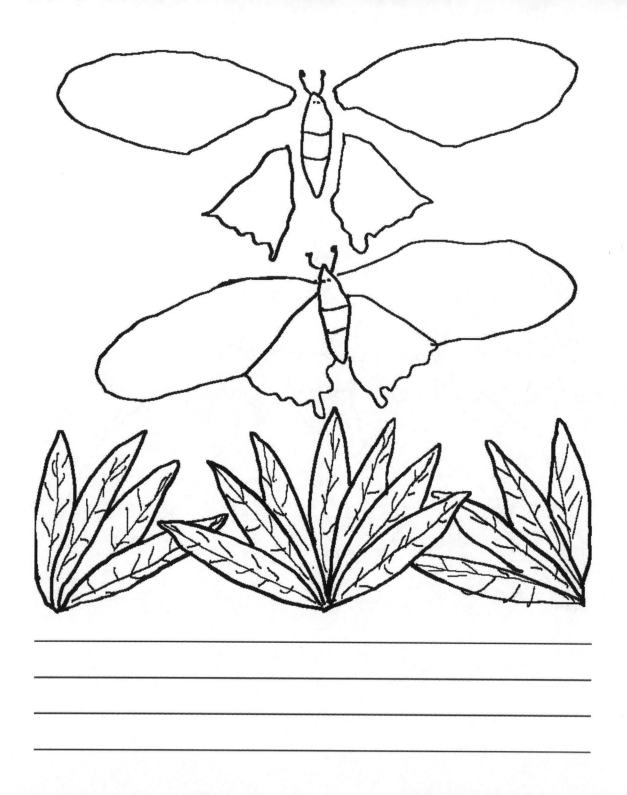

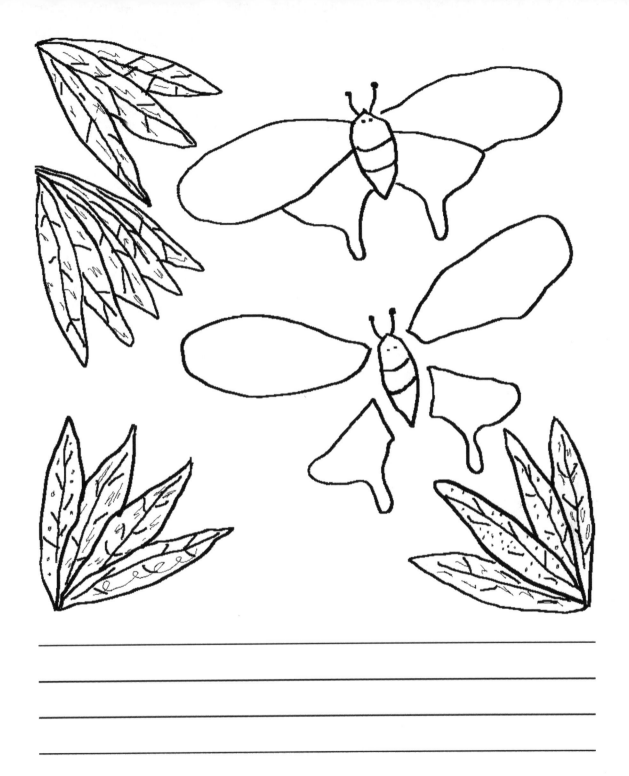

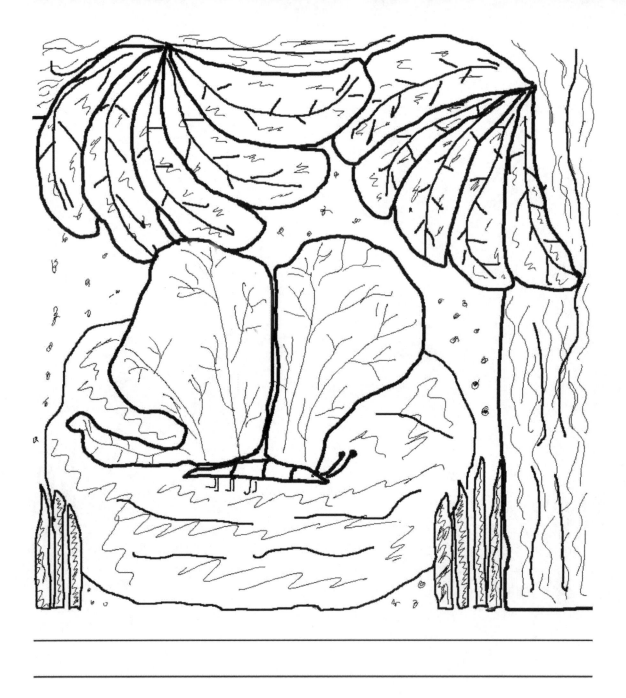

_____

_____

_____

_____

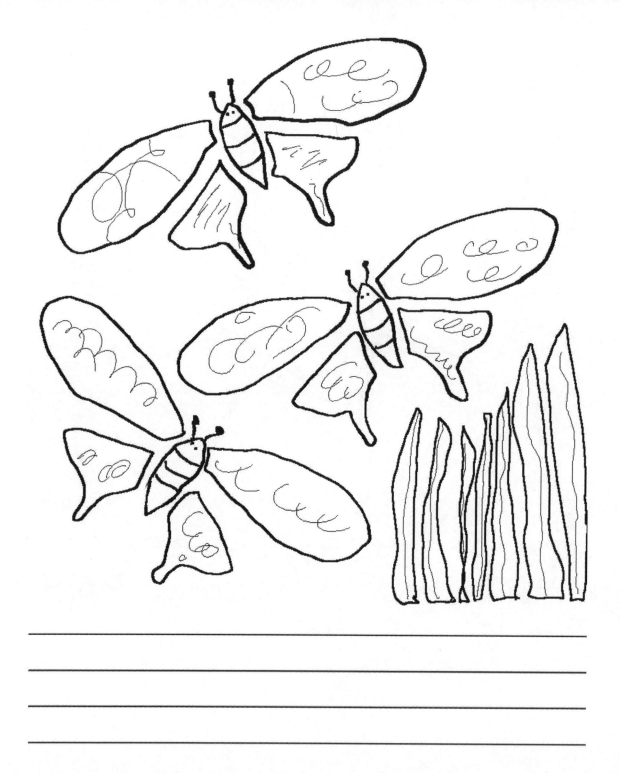

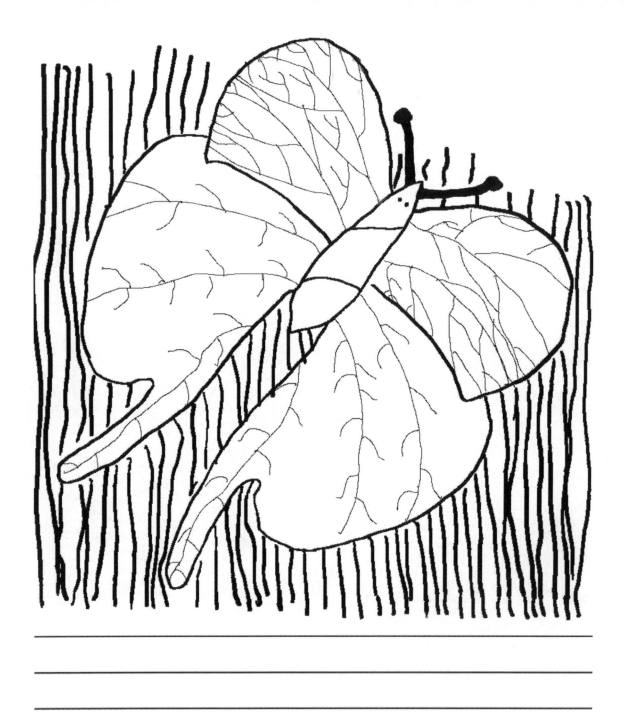

_____

_____

_____

_____

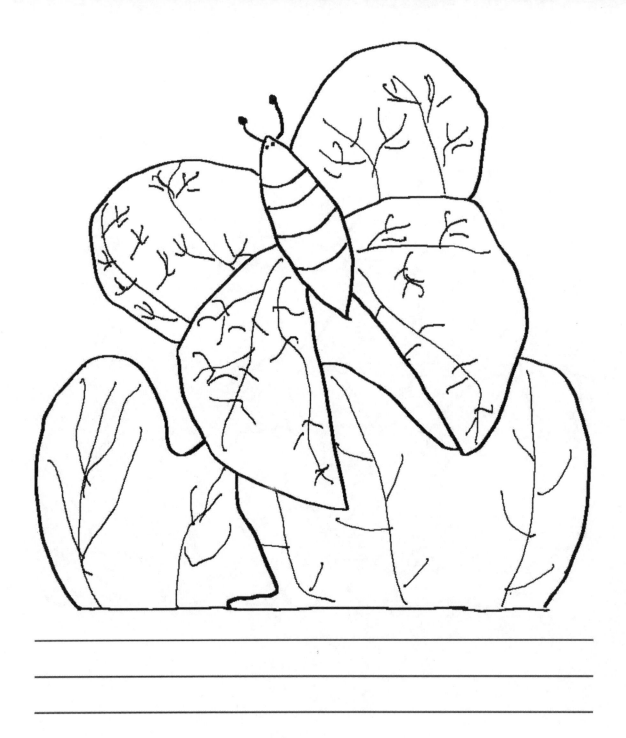

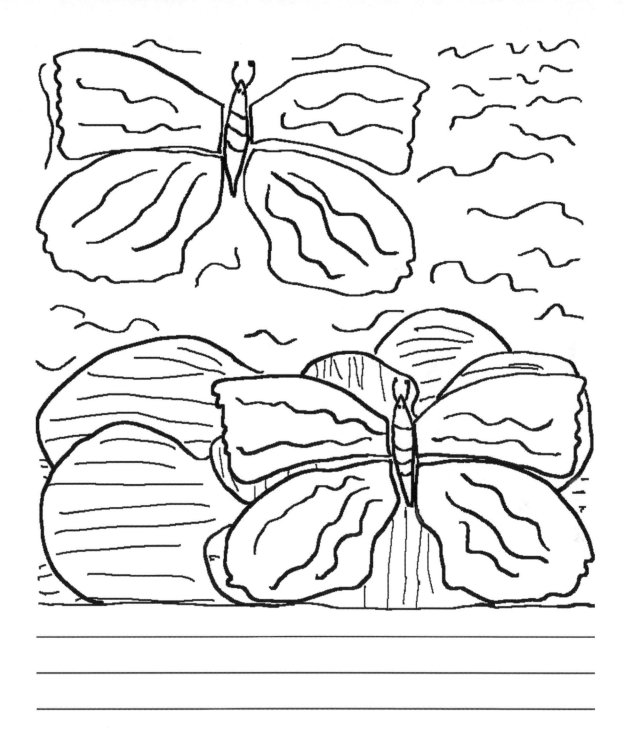

_____

_____

_____

_____

Draw, color and write your own Haiku

Draw, color and write your own Haiku

Draw, color and write your own Haiku

Draw, color and write your own Haiku

Draw, color and write your own Haiku

Butterfly Haiku Coloring Book
by
Jacquelyn Jaie Fourgerel

ISBN-13: 978-1545253496

ISBN-10: 1545253498

www.jacquelynjaiefourgerel.com

E-mail: jfourgerel@gmail.com

Copyright: 2017 Jacquelyn Jaie Fourgerel.
All Rights Reserved.

Printed by: Kindle Direct Publishing, 2017

No part of this book may be reproduced, stored in a retrieval system, or transmitted by any means without the written permission of the author.

Made in the USA
Middletown, DE
20 September 2024